This
Prue Theobalds Book
belongs to

_____

_____

_____

_____

_____

*For Roxanne, Kio, Jacob and Jess*
P. T.

First published in hardback in 1994
by David Bennett Books Ltd,
94 Victoria Street, St Albans,
Herts AL1 3TG.

First published in paperback in 1995
by David Bennett Books Ltd

This edition published by Uplands Books in 1995
1 The Uplands, Maze Hill, St Leonards-on-Sea,
East Sussex TN38 0HL, United Kingdom.

BRITISH LIBRARY
CATALOGUING-IN-PUBLICATION DATA
A catalogue record for this book is available
from the British Library.

ISBN 1 897951 09 4

Typesetting by Goodfellow and Egan
Production by Imago
Printed in China

Prue Theobalds'

# Book of Busy Bears

A pot-pourri of visual games

David Bennett Books

# C o n t

I'm Bertie

I'm Boris

I'm Brenda

I'm Billy

I'm Belle

ents

I'm Bess

I'm Bertha

I'm Bobby

I'm Ben

I'm Belinda

# Good-morning Bears!

Wake up bears!
Time to start your busy day!

Do you know all the bears' names?

9

# Keep-fit Bears

Every day the bears do their exercises,
so they will grow up strong and healthy
and not too tubby!  Today, Boris is the leader.
When he does an exercise, the other bears
have to copy him.

Boris tells the bears to . . .

stretch up to the sky

hop on one leg

do a handstand

touch their toes

spin like a top     jump high in the air     twist right round

**Which exercises are Brenda, Billy and Bertha doing?**

run on the spot             bounce like a ball

Poor Ben has had enough!

# Bear Weather

Each morning, the bears look out
of the window to see what
the weather is like.

Can you help the bears choose their clothes
for different kinds of weather?

Sometimes it is sunny.

Sometimes it is rainy.

Sometimes it is windy.

Sometimes it snows!

13

# I Spy Colours . . .

Today, the weather is bright and sunny.
The bears are enjoying themselves
in the garden.  Some of them
are playing I Spy.

I spy things that are yellow

Help the bears spy
their favourite colours.

15

# Rocket to the Moon

Bobby and Ben are very adventurous.
They are planning a trip to the moon.
But first, they need to build a rocket.
They have asked all the other bears to help.

What have they used
to build their rocket?

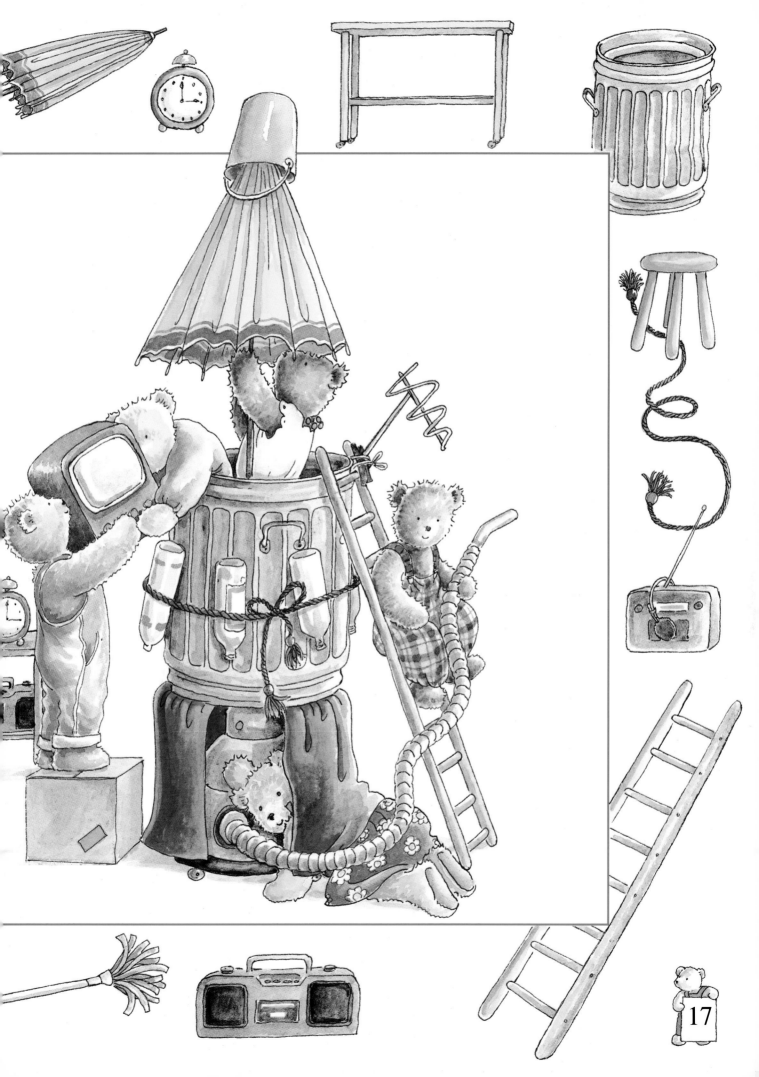

17

# Spot the Ball

The bears are all playing
different ball games.
Brenda and Billy are playing catch.

Who has the biggest ball?
Who has the smallest ball?
How many balls
can you see altogether?

Look out
Belle!

# Lost and Found

While the young bears play,
the grown-ups go to work.
But each of these silly bears
has lost something.  Can you find
all the things they have lost?

Belinda's cousin
is a postman.
What has he lost?

Bertha's daddy
is a fisherman.
What has he lost?

Bobby's sister
is a hairdresser.
What has she lost?

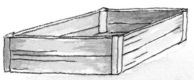

Billy's mummy
is a farmer.
What has she lost?

flowers

letters

Ben's granny
sells flowers.
What has she lost?

brush

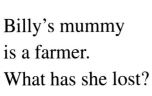

bread

fish

Bess's uncle
is a baker.
What has he lost?

sheep

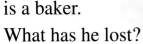

21

# Little Bear Lost

Poor Brenda is lost in the maze.
She cannot find her way out.
Her friends are trying to help.
Can you trace the way
out of the maze with your finger?

# Bertie's Birthday

Today is Bertie's birthday!
He is having a party and the others
are giving him presents.

These are Bertie's presents.
Can you guess which present
was in which parcel?

# Park Playtime

Maggie
the mouse

Digger
the dog

The teddy bears go to the playground.
They meet lots of their friends there.

Bruce
the bunny

Here are the teddies' friends.
Can you see them in the big picture?

26

Chester
the cat

Dotty
the doll

Oscar
the owl

Maurice
the monkey

Max
the mouse

27

# A Skipping Puzzle

The bears love skipping,
but their ropes have become tangled.
Can you help?
Follow each rope with your finger
to find out which two bears
are holding each rope.

29

# Teddy Bears' Picnic

The bears are having a picnic beside the lake. They have brought some wonderful things to eat!

Look at all the good things
on the picnic rug. Now shut
your eyes – how many
of them can you remember?

31

# Which Way, Bears?

The bears are looking at a map
to find their way home.
There are two different paths.
Bobby and Boris are arguing
about which one is the shortest.

Bears' Home

Can you show them the shortest path from the lake with your finger?

# Hide and Seek

On their way home, the bears
walk through a wood.
'Let's play hide and seek!' says Belle.
'I'll count to ten, and you hide!'

This is the bears' favourite game.
They love hiding!

Count to ten with Belle.
Then help her to find the other bears.

# Flying Kites

It's getting very windy!
Brenda, Bertie, Bess and Boris
are trying to fly their kites,
but all the strings are tangled.

Follow each string with your finger.
Which kite belongs to which bear?

37

# Blustery Bears

Oh no!  Ben's hat, Bobby's scarf
and Brenda's kite have all blown away.
Luckily they have not gone far.

This is what the missing things
look like.  Can you see them
hidden in the big picture?

# Fancy Dress Bears

When they get home, the bears
open the dressing-up box.
Belinda, Boris and Billy
have to guess what the others
are pretending to be.

Can you guess too?

# Too Many Cooks

Ben's colander

Belle's oven gloves

Bobby's rolling-pin

The bears are getting hungry, but there are so many of them in the kitchen that they cannot find everything they need.

Here are all the things the bears need. Can you find them in the big picture?

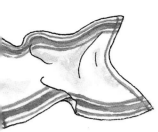 Boris's tea towel

 Billy's cookery book

 Bertha's frying pan

 Belinda's cake tin

 Brenda's whisk

 Bess's beaker

 Bertie's spoon

 43

# Good-night Bears!

What a busy day!
The bears are all very sleepy.
Bess starts to read a bedtime story.

Soon all our busy bears are fast asleep!

Other Prue Theobalds titles published by Uplands Books which will keep you busy . . .

Pressout Books

**I Saw A Ship A-Sailing**     *ISBN 0 9512246 7 0*

**Teddy Bears' Picnic**     *ISBN 0 9512246 8 9*

**Old MacDonald Had A Farm**     *ISBN 1 897951 02 7*

**Theo's Dressing Up Box**     *ISBN 1 897951 03 5*

**Theo's Wonderful Flying Machine**     *ISBN 1 897951 04 3*

and her Picture Book

**The Bears' Seaside Adventure**     *Hardback ISBN 0 9512246 6 2*

*Paperback ISBN 0 9512246 5 4*